lofts

a style of living

Original editions in French, English, Spanish, Italian

Translation by Translate-A-Book, Oxford

Design and creation : GRAPH'M

ISBN: 2-7528-0070-3
Publisher code : T00070

Copyright registration: October 2004

Printed in Singapore by Tien Wah Press

www.fitwaypublishing.com

Fitway Publishing
12, avenue d'Italie – 75627 Paris cedex 13

archiDesign

lofts
a style of living

élodie piveteau and caroline wietzel

fitway
publishing

contents

Introduction

Radically changing lifestyles, the increasing growth of towns and financial considerations are among the disparate factors that influence and help determine where and how we live today. The proliferation of lofts and the increasing popularity of loft living are phenomena of our age. At the same time, the development of residential lofts has emerged as a prime method of preserving and safeguarding our rich architectural heritage.

The notion of living in buildings previously used by industry originated in the 1950s and has been growing in popularity ever since. Back in those early days, lofts were cheap, cheerful and Bohemian; today, they are expensive, luxurious and more often the prerogative of a well-heeled elite. Loft living proclaims a quality of life based on a sense of space and spaciousness. In short, the loft is a blank canvas on which original features and innovative design can be successfully combined according to personal choice.

New York in the 1950s. The first lofts appeared in Manhattan.

'Thanksgiving 1945. Eric's place was an apartment-cum-hallway in a Sullivan-designed building. For me, it had Bohemian chic in spades – like Eric himself: bath in the kitchen, Chianti bottles converted into lamp bases, tired old cushions scattered around on the floor, and books, books, books everywhere. This was Greenwich Village way before the Beatnik era. Eric was definitely ahead of his time ...'[1]

To understand why, only a few years later, this 'bohemian chic' was all the rage, it is essential to look at the **historical dimension**.

1 - Douglas Kennedy: *In Search of Happiness*, Editions Pocket 2003, p. 116.

With their brick walls and metal framework, industrial façades hide new ways of living.

Loft living had its beginnings in New York City in the 1950s when the middle classes started deserting Manhattan in droves, fleeing the crowds and the pollution and heading for single-family peace and domesticity in the suburbs. Meanwhile, the art crowd was starting to move into run-down and disused industrial buildings, attracted by the prospect of ample space to live and work and, not least, by affordable rents.

Zoom in on the area South of Houston, now known as SoHo. Here's where it all *really* started. Around 1950

The cast-iron frame industrial buildings of the 19th century house the first lofts.

or so, workshops and warehouses were left empty as obsolete plant shut down for good or moved to more modern out-of-town facilities. Left behind in this process of **disindustrialisation** was a plethora of real estate dating from the latter half of the nineteenth century: multi-storey factory and warehouse premises with vast open-plan surface areas, built to conventional American industrial design specifications, typically with non-bearing iron-frame 'curtain' façades and generous expanses of windows.

The move to South Houston was born out of **economic necessity**. Artists forced out of Greenwich Village by spiralling rents sought refuge in its spacious and airy buildings, where they could live and work for next to nothing. A description of Robert Rauschenberg's studio in Fulton Street in the very heart of 1953 Manhattan is enough to send shivers down the spine: 'A huge attic space with twenty-foot high ceilings. No heat. No running water. The rent was fifteen dollars a month but Rauschenberg haggled it down to ten. A down pipe and a bucket in the backyard masqueraded as a sink and Rauschenberg took clandestine showers at friends' houses, asking to go to the can, then taking a shower in double-quick time.'[1]

1 - Sharon Zukin: *Loft Living: Culture and Capital in Urban Changes*, Rutgers University Press, 1989, p. 61.

OLIVER'S WHARF.
LIVER'S
WHARF

The advent of this new breed of tenant represented a modest windfall for the owners of disused and dilapidated buildings. Some, at least, managed to earn a modicum of return on their property pending the (apparently inevitable) demolition order. Meanwhile, New York City's Urban Planning Commission had kept a watchful eye on what was happening in South Houston. The original notion had been to tear down the old buildings to make room for a new urban expressway. But the powers-that-be had second thoughts: they retained Professor Chester Rapkin to investigate the area's status quo and assess its economic potential. Rapkin's findings, published in 1963, were revealing and decisive. The bottom line was that, far from being deserted and semi-derelict, South Houston was economically alive and well, with a viable economy that looked set to expand, offsetting the middle class exodus to the suburbs. Rapkin's report also highlighted the importance many people attached to these cast-iron frame buildings as an integral part of the city's **heritage**.

The upshot was a campaign to save them from demolition. The New York City 'loft phenomenon' had taken cultural root. It would be copied elsewhere in major industrial conurbations such as London and Berlin, where factories and warehouses were deemed an important component of the national heritage and were gradually transformed into living space.

Mains water pipes, electric ducting and supporting pillars become part of the décor of a living space that is largely open.

The first wave of tenants comprised artists, painters, writers, sculptors, dancers, choreographers, students, university lecturers and 'intellectuals'. For them, this was essentially a **politically subversive** statement. For starters, their chosen mode of living was tantamount to rejection of the prevailing model of the day, that of the 1960s middle class whose concept of social success – of having 'made it' – was a suburban home with a manicured lawn and a white picket fence. This revolt against what were widely perceived as *petit bourgeois* values resulted over time in a re-investment in the inner city. Moreover, initially many lofts were occupied 'unofficially', in other words they were illegal squats. In New York City, numerous groups such as the SoHo Artists Association, the Artists Tenant Association or the Association for Artists' Housing,[1] lobbied for statutory reform. In the event, the first bye-laws voted in New York City in 1964 likened artists to 'light industry' and required them to register their tenancies accordingly. Lofts were thus granted recognition in the eyes of the law. In the space of a single year, over 3,000 artists duly registered.

1 - Anne Dressen: *Le Monde de l'art new-yorkais en quête d'alternatives. Avant-garde et espaces d'exposition – 1950/1980. Ethnographie d'une contestation,* mémoire de DEA, Université Paris I, 2001. *(The New York Art World in Search of Alternatives. The Avant-Garde and Exhibition Space 1950/1980, An Ethnographic Confrontation, DEA memorandum, Paris University, 2001).*

A **new mode of urban living** had come of age. In part, it was modelled on the vie de Bohème espoused by European artists who descended on nineteenth-century Paris to live and work in garrets and attics in Montmartre and Montparnasse, eking out a living on the fringes of society certainly, but also making a productive and innovative contribution to the world around them.

In essence, the loft was non-conformist and 'different'. It represented a utopian community peopled by a creative and non-conventional avant-garde. To put it another way, 'SoHo's run-down appearance of unalleviated poverty and disorder had an implicit psycho-social resonance that was perceived as a warranty for moral integrity and as a rejection of base monetary considerations. Artists and 'Bohemians' had annexed the inner city and SoHo now offered them a new *modus vivendi* in the guise of loft living.'[1]

In physical terms, the absence of dividing walls abolished the traditional distinction between living space and work space. The loft became a venue nurtured by a sense of freedom and spatial mobility. Andy Warhol's celebrated

1 - *Op. cit.*

Originally at the heart of the town but now on the outskirts, industrial buildings have become a place in their own right.

'Factory' (a term that perhaps says it all) was arguably the most potent emblem of this new 'rock'n'roll' phenomenon. There, behind the silvery façade on Union Square, new artistic movements were spawned, new groups created, new films directed, new 'happenings' improvised. Over time, they were destined to become the stuff of legend.

The loft was a space in which to live *and* work, but it was also a place to **exhibit**. There was a fundamental correlation between the space itself and the artistic output it facilitated. Avant-garde aspirations to reconcile 'art' and 'life' found full expression in these vast floor areas that were still redolent of sweat-shop exploitation. Above all, however, the space itself was tailor-made for outsize-format canvases and, not least, for 'installations' and 'happenings'. The loft challenged the conventional notion of the art gallery. The space was no longer a mere passive receptacle for people and objects but, instead, an active participant, a 'player' in the creative act itself. Loft and artist became as one. And art dealers were quick to realise this and climb on the bandwagon.

During the 1970s, the loft revealed its potential as a **profitable market** for the art world generally. Industrial premises lying fallow in metropolitan areas were gradually converted and, from Chicago to New Orleans (by way of Paris, Manchester and Barcelona), the craze persisted for the better part of a decade. By the 1980s, the loft had already become a status symbol – the supreme irony being that this once-marginalised, anti-authoritarian and 'alternative' lifestyle was now a *sine qua non* of incipient yuppiedom.

As real estate markets boomed in the 1980s, the **progressive middle-class takeover** of loft culture was trumpeted in the media. Artists who had cashed in on their celebrity status posed in resplendent loft conversions for full-page spreads in glossy magazines. The process had, in a sense, come full circle: the alienated artist had been elevated to the status of cultural icon. Loft living was now a *must*, as Sharon Zukin and others have pointed out: 'These studios were around for years but nobody ever thought it would be chic to live in them'.[1] All this inevitably prompts the question: now that loft living is associated in most people's minds with a moneyed social elite, has the loft lost its soul?

1 - Sharon Zukin: *Loft Living: Culture and Capital in Urban Changes*, Rutgers University Press, 1989, p. 14.

Lofts have become a middle-class commodity; they are both a symbol of a bygone age and a contemporary way of living.

In these open living spaces, 'rooms' and their functions are only defined by metallic structures and by furniture.

The Sword of Damocles is no longer poised and loft-dwellers no longer live under the threat of eviction. Today, they can afford to expend their time and energy on embellishing their properties. This constitutes fertile territory for interior designers (not to mention substantial revenue in terms of fees). Lofts have acquired new terms of reference. Once doggedly anti-establishment, they went on to become 'cool', 'fashionable' and 'switched on', emerging ultimately as a positive contributory factor to urban life and urban renewal. Not least, lofts have imparted new life and a new aesthetic to old materials and have generated a fresh appreciation of industrial design by highlighting architectural gems hitherto concealed from view behind stark and unprepossessing façades. In effect, the loft has returned to its roots, demonstrating that beauty is very much in the eye of the beholder and that some features reveal their intrinsic beauty and charm not instantly but only slowly and after a painstaking process of exploration and analysis.

The loft is no longer a stand-alone phenomenon. Its **influence** has spread to and impacted on the interior design of galleries, bars, restaurants and boutiques. Paradoxically, the loft phenomenon that breathed new life into sections of New York's inner city in the 1960s has now moved beyond the city centre and into the once-maligned suburbs; as inner-city rents soar, the 'industrial look' has made its mark in areas such as Brooklyn in New York City (and, for that matter, around the inner suburban belt in Greater London).

Lofts mutate, lofts adapt, lofts re-invent themselves incessantly. As a result, their **definition** has also evolved. Once, a loft was no more and no less than the top floor of a factory or warehouse. When lofts began to

be converted to commercial use in the 1950s, however, a 'loft' was redefined to mean any area used originally for industrial or commercial purposes and subsequently fitted out as a living space. Ever since the first conversions in New York, urban sites in many cities have been designated 'lofts', ranging from the cast-iron structures in New York City itself to the glass roof-top *ateliers* of Paris and the brick warehouses on the banks of the Thames in London.

Demand soon exceeded supply to the point where the term 'loft' was no longer restricted to converted nineteenth century industrial buildings but was expanded to apply to all manner of more recent premises, such as schools, offices and even boats. Conventional apartments are now being converted to 'loft-style' living areas. In a nutshell, the word 'loft' has not only taken on a new meaning, it has also engendered a new style and image. It is quite common these days to find large apartments featuring open-plan living spaces unencumbered by interior partitions. The original SoHo loft has become a brand that is both specific and generic. As Francis Nordemann, architect and principal of the College of Architecture in Normandy (France) has noted, 'When I design an apartment block, I always regret the fact that partitioning off individual areas tends to rob the spatial volumes of their intrinsic interest, particularly when the building in question has double or even triple exposure. When such apartments are left in their 'raw' state, they have all the hallmarks of new lofts with large, free-flowing surfaces extending unimpeded from one façade to the other.'

In China the loft has retained its primary role as a place for artistic production.

In other words, the **absence of dividing walls** (or, to be more precise, *conventional* partitions) is essentially what sets the loft apart from other types of living space. The loft boasts an inner space that is fluid, supple, frequently modular, a space for work and play that can metamorphose at will and as those living in it see fit.

The notion of **large space** is intrinsic to the loft concept, but that too is undergoing a process of change. Sharon Zukin's descriptions of loft buildings in SoHo routinely cite floor areas of between 200 and 1,000 m^2 and, by convention, a loft should boast a surface area in excess of that lower figure. But escalating real estate prices in major urban centres have led to the genesis of the 'mini-loft', a term used to describe surface areas of a modest 100 m^2 or even 30 m^2. When all is said and done, this seems little more than a marketing ploy, with the original loft concept diluted to connote nothing more than a 'well-organised space'.

The loft phenomenon was originally firmly anchored in North America and Europe, but has now been exported to all four corners of the earth. Major cities in North America and Europe were in the vanguard of those playing host to the first loft *aficionados*, and examples of loft living are legion from Chicago to Milan by way of London, Brussels, Paris and elsewhere. In some countries, however, local statutes and regulations blocked the development of lofts; certain countries – Canada and Finland immediately spring to mind – had to wait until the 1990s before embracing the loft concept fully. Since then, in Montreal and Quebec alone, sales of loft-style dwellings have nearly doubled in the space of 15 years.

The 798, an old factory north of Beijing, combines galleries, creative spaces and private living areas.

注意安全

The loft approach is also making headway in South America although, for cultural and economic reasons, the pace of development is comparatively slow. In Brazil's São Paulo, for example, the vast majority of industrial buildings are virtual ruins and, worse, are located as a rule in dangerous, no-go areas of the city. Remarkably, it is in the Far East that the most spectacular changes appear to be taking place. China – a country whose concern for architectural heritage has, over the years, been less than overwhelming (to put it mildly) – is starting to sit up and take notice. There, the population at large is mobilising its efforts at the local level to safeguard the urban environment[1]. Investment in gigantic disused factory buildings is proceeding apace as Chinese artists exploit new-found freedom from censorship to re-invent their lifestyles. Loft living is increasingly common on the fringes of China's main cities, reminiscent of the innovative and 'subversive' movement that, by contrast, spread out from the centre of New York City in the 1950s. The loft concept is making major inroads in a country where space is at a premium, but loft living in China is not without risk: the spectre of compulsory eviction looms large and even '798', the former electronic components manufacturing facility northwest of Beijing which was converted into galleries, shops and living space, is under threat from the bulldozer. That said, some Chinese artists who have made their name in the international marketplace have already set up city-centre studios in designer lofts. It may be that yet another cultural revolution is about to take place.

1 - *Courrier international*, September 19, 2002.

The loft: space for living and for creating and exhibiting one's work.

Very high ceilings and zenithal light … you have to work within the architectural constraints.

A tailor-made conversion: dividing the space up in a way that adapts what is there to the needs of the inhabitants.

Loft lingo

Apertures

Industrial buildings generally feature a wide variety of openings to the exterior; the goal is to optimise the ample light resources available by the most effective arrangement of space and materials.

Structure

This defines the loft and its personality; bear-ng elements (metal frame, support beams, ducting and so on) are frequently left exposed or sometimes clad, but are always highlighted n some way to underpin the industrial prov-enance and 'feel' of the original building.

Separations

These are kept to a minimum and used exclu-sively to allocate space and to preserve the intimate nature of certain 'zones of privacy' such as bedrooms or bathrooms.

Recycling

This is the process of integrating existing elements into a new interior design without damaging the original features or changing their roles.

Flexibility

Tinkering with spatial volumes to adapt them to specific needs and preferences; thus, movable dividers help break up space to meet the occupier's current needs.

Multi-functional

A key loft characteristic and a major plus: a large surface area is structured so as to allow a range of varied activities to take place at the same time.

Finish

A successful marriage between the original structure in its unimproved state and the very smooth minimalist design features subsequently imported.

ʼlaterialisation

ı the absence of dividers/partitions, usable urface area is defined in terms of 'zones of ctivity'; a change in materials used, or the position of an item of furniture may be sufficient to lelineate a zone.

Loft. design

Lofts come in various shapes and guises that reflect the intent behind the original design and the tastes and preferences of their current occupants. The earliest lofts in New York were often left 'as is', but things have moved on considerably since the 1950s when the architect Smith-Miller would revamp buildings for a fee that often amounted to little more than a pack of cigarettes or a bottle of Scotch, saying, 'Fact is, you couldn't do anything with the walls, they were in such a rotten state. The best you could do was add a column or two or build in a few features.'[1]

It didn't take long, however, for middle-class values to reassert themselves. Loft owners became more demanding in terms of creature comforts and progressively sophisticated design features. Interior designers also made their mark, overturning some basic precepts in the process. Nevertheless, certain fundamental tenets continued to apply in terms of how space could be defined and orchestrated without infringing the original building design.

A new building is designed to order, but the loft *re*-designer must live with a number of constraints and make a virtue out of certain necessities. First off, a loft design has to take full account of the original space and the use for which it was intended. A loft is 'converted' and, as

such – as Francis Nordemann stresses – must therefore 'survive beyond the use for which it was originally created'. This means that the 'converters' must be mindful of architectural heritage generally, irrespective of whether they are restoring old farmhouses, making a school out of a former factory or creating a cultural centre in an erstwhile public building. A notable example of such conversions are the *Public School I* project in Queens, New York, where a museum was fashioned from an old school building, and the Musée d'Orsay in Paris, which was installed in a decommissioned railway station.

A loft must retain a distinct **historical footprint,** as architect James Soane insists when he declares, 'A loft is not simply an empty space – its history is intrinsic to its design and, as such, must be brought out and validated'.[2]

1 - Marcus Field, Mark Irving: *Lofts*, Seuil, 1999, p. 43.
2 - *Op. cit.*, p. 45.

Opposite: *The original building imposes its own rules. Here the staircase winds around a supporting pillar.*

Above: *The height creates extra space. A mezzanine floor often provides an ideal solution.*

A loft is often identified by a combination of old and new features.

The fundamental consideration is the need to respect the use to which the loft was put in a previous existence and to utilise features which render that previous existence more or less explicit. Preserving this historical envelope enables a clear distinction between the old and the new; it also imparts **value to the industrial dimension** by retaining **evidence of the raw materials** used specifically in the construction process (beams, columns and the like) rather than highlighting design features added during the conversion.

A living space, a working space – the distinction between the two has disappeared.

The urban style is retained, preserving the building's past history.

1 - *Op. cit.*, p. 146.
2 - Sharon Zukin: *Loft Living: Culture and Capital in Urban Changes*, Rutgers University Press, 1989, p. 59.

For a time, there was a distinct wave of **nostalgia** when it came to preserving original artefacts such as loading bays, pulleys, cisterns and so forth but, come the 1970s, those features were generally felt to be more trouble than they were worth. Painter and photographer Dieter Kramer, a pioneering loft-dweller in Berlin, recalls:

'The lofts in those days were bursting at the seams with bits of old machinery and whatever. Maybe that would be considered "chic" these days, but back then we simply threw all that stuff out?[1]

It remains to be seen whether or not today's loft dwellers still pursue what Sharon Zukin[2] has termed 'the modern quest for authenticity' – of which the loft is the incarnation *par excellence* – or whether that authenticity is simply a question of shrewd marketing. What is certain is that many estate agents now freely admit that in the boom years of the 1990s they unashamedly packed their promotional literature with photographs of what they described as 'genuine', 'original' and 'authentic' features in a bid to market a particular lifestyle. Others reluctantly concede that this 'authenticity' was achieved in some instances by the expedient use of 'authentic' features imported into so-called 'lofts' that were actually constructed from scratch in brand new buildings. Like many of his fellow architects, Renato Benedetti rails against this practice saying, 'Very often, what you see is completely superficial. A hoist that has been cleaned up but is never used is simply a token, a fetish. But photographing and promoting it in a flashy prospectus as an 'authentic' feature, *that* is a downright disgrace.'

Lofts are subject to **intrinsic structural constraints**. Francis Nordemann points out that 'the architect's first task when working on a loft is not only to identify and highlight its positive features but also to pinpoint its existing drawbacks and work out how to

Particular aspects of the building are consciously made into features. Here, a wooden and stripped beams create a particular atmosphere.

overcome them.' Smith-Miller notes that, from the word 'go', a loft is a **space to be 'filled'**, adding that the architect has to 'squat' the space concerned and 'intervene' in its development. In essence, the original function of the space and of its structural elements must be taken as the point of departure: they are the theme tune around which the rest of the design score is composed.

What is totally out of the question is to re-create and impose the functions of a conventional apartment. In this respect, the loft mania that began during the 1990s has most definitely muddied the waters: 'chic' and 'trendy' loft living was media-hyped to such a degree that many people were lured into the mistaken belief that this would be their ideal lifestyle when, in reality, that was emphatically *not* the case. The paradox is that they then proceeded to fit out their loft as they would have done a conventional apartment – re-converting a loft conversion, as it were – more often than not with disastrous results. As James Soane has said, 'You have to make your mind up and go for one thing or the other. It is nothing short of scandalous when somebody moves into a loft and then starts fixing it up like a suburban property – complete with three bedrooms, two bathrooms, a kitchen-diner and what have you, all neatly wall-papered. When an architect takes on a loft conversion, the last thing on his mind is to end up with a cute little house in the 'burbs. Working on a loft is a whole different ball game. It's like working on a three-dimensional puzzle.'[1]

1 - Marcus Field-Mark Irving: *Lofts*, Seuil, 1999, p. 138.

Although some might detect the merest hint of snobbery in the above statement, all it does in reality is point out the distinction between one genre and another. Francis Nordemann sees a loft 'as a spatial volume with objects floating in it'. Diane Lewis, who lectures on architecture and is herself a practising architect, endorses this view when she observes that loft living implies an architecture that is 'long-range' in the sense that 'the objects of day-to-day existence – kitchen, bedroom, bathroom – become furniture'.[1]

What this adds up to is a permutation of practical and aesthetic considerations. Thus, a key component of loft living is the seamless continuity that should exist between the living and working space on the one hand and its basic constituent features on the other, taking into account their compatibility with the profession, lifestyle, tastes and preferences of the individual occupant(s). Moreover, in the case of a loft, the 'practical and aesthetic considerations' are far removed from those that apply to a conventional dwelling. The loft is, above all, a *different* kind of space, a space that departs from the domestic norm in that it re-assigns and redistributes priorities and establishes a fresh set of hierarchies.

The notion of **separate zones** within a continuous and unbroken space is both fundamental and problematic. In the early days of the loft, the tendency was to put everything on an equal footing and to reject any hint of partitions or dividers. The perceived need for separate spaces is linked in part to the gradual middle-class takeover of loft lifestyles. Irrespective of whether the loft dweller is a pioneer or a recent convert, however, the trend has been towards progressive use of divider elements, more often than not for reasons of day-to-day family life.

The need to create zones is also dictated in part by the twin considerations of noise and heating, two major problems which beset loft life. But the need for **intimacy** is also an issue. In practice, offices, bedrooms and bathrooms in a conventional home will typically be closed off and/or soundproofed whereas, in a loft, they more often than not remain open. As it happens, many architects and interior designers are vehemently opposed to creating 'rooms' in a loft as if it were a conventional apartment or house, so much so that one London-based architect is on record as having said, 'Rather than building a closed-off room in a loft, I'd plant a garden shed slap-bang in the middle of it'. Francis

1 *Op. cit.*, p. 43.

The bathroom opens out on to the communal area. A scene of intimacy.

Openness is all-important. The spaces open up and close off according to need.

Nordemann's attitude is more restrained in this respect, but he, too, seriously questions 'the unseemly haste to install mezzanines', adding that, 'in the long run, creating a new surface area disrupts the overall feeling of space and is the first step on the road back towards a conventional apartment'. Like his London counterpart, Nordemann would opt for other, more imaginative solutions – even perhaps 'installing a tent'.

It has to be said that changing space does not necessarily imply the use of partitions: an array of beams, a step, a slightly-raised area or a different floor covering can work equally well, if not better. Installing a mezzanine is a recurrent solution, however, and it must be conceded that it does semi-isolate a private zone and provide additional surface area.

Overall, the increasing need for additional space marked an important stage in the development of loft culture and has led to a number of interesting variants, not least in the use of dividers placed at a tangent to the wall or arranged in a curve or zigzag. An important and obvious constraint is with regard to natural light. Dividers should in any event stop short of the ceiling, and blind spots should be avoided, typically by the use of slits in the dividers themselves or by using transparent or translucent materials that allow the light to be diffused more evenly.

Loft mobility is more than a buzzword: unlike a conventional house, where the various rooms and functions are predetermined and immutable, the loft space thrives on flexibility and multiple use. Accordingly, sliding doors that are fully retractable are often a feature, as are easily moved dividers, both of which enable the various zones to be redefined at will. By the same token, furniture is frequently placed on castors or rails; even if it is moved infrequently (or never), this helps create and intensify a 'functional' look for, as Philippe Starck has rightly remarked, 'mobility and modularity are more a state of mind than a functional reality'.[1]

The concept of **misappropriation** is paramount at every level. This is no more than a logical follow-up to the initial premise of loft development, namely that an industrial space can be 're-routed' for loft living. The principal evidence of such misappropriation is to be found in the materials that decorate the typical loft, such as industrial quality installations that were never designed for domestic use and exposed pipes, ducts and cabling that would – under 'normal' circumstances – be concealed either by being covered or by being built into the walls. Various objects in the loft may also be misappropriated to the extent that they are put to uses other than those for which they were originally designed: bookcases become zone dividers, goods lifts metamorphose into dressing-rooms, metal office files are stacked to make a wardrobe, and unusual furniture is created by subverting an item's original use, so that a petrol pump becomes a kitchen feature, supermarket trolleys mutate into shelving, and so on.

1 - François Bellanger: *Habitat(s): Questions et hypothèses sur l'évolution de l'habitat* ('Habitat(s): Questions and Hypotheses on the Evolution of the Human Habitat'), Éditions de l'Aube, 2000, p. 15.

A town aspect and a garden aspect: the living space always opens up to the outside.

The loft-dweller's **aesthetic sense** plays a key role. There is ample room for manoeuvre in this respect and a single loft can be fitted out in so many different, not to say diametrically opposed ways. For example, tiled floors and wooden beams are traditionally associated with a rustic look, and waxing or varnishing them merely reinforces and enhances that look, whereas painting them white will tend to make them appear somehow more sophisticated.
Equally, a stripped-down, refined, **minimalist** look is achieved by emphasising spatial volumes and by *de*-emphasising furnishings and equipment. To the extent that white walls, light wooden floors and soft surfaces are currently all the rage, floors these days tend to be sanded down and/or coated and walls are rubbed or skimmed to effect a smooth finish. This approach is highly reminiscent of that adopted by art museums and galleries, where the room is effectively erased in order to throw its contents into sharper relief.
Another approach entirely is the purist, **natural** and bohemian look, where the motto is, quite literally, 'Let it all hang out'. Nothing is hidden, everything is on view: raw bricks are left exposed, support columns are stripped of their cladding, false ceilings are ripped down, and heating, water and electrical ducts and circuits are left in full view.
The final décor is also a matter of personal taste. Theatre-style with *trompe l'oeil* flourishes? Exotic, with virgin forest scenes? Japanese screens? Kitsch with *chinoiseries*? Whatever – these and other variations on the loft theme

1 - Marcus Field, Mark Irving: *Lofts*, Seuil, 1999, p. 141.
2 - François Bellanger: *Habitat(s): Questions et hypothèses sur l'évolution de l'habitat* ('Habitat(s): Questions and Hypotheses on the Evolution of the Human Habitat'), Éditions de l'Aube, 2000, p. 15.

are a far cry from the monochrome modalities of yesteryear with their mandatory glass bricks, exposed concrete and Le Corbusier chair. Modern classics remain a benchmark, however, and have tended to turn loft aesthetics into a **cliché**: 'With every option open to them to re-invent their lifestyles', says James Soane, 'people still persist in painting everything white and acquiring a few items of carefully-selected furniture. In the process, they make a travesty out of the loft genre.'[1]

It should be added that certain objects from the world of industry now belong in the must-have category: a stainless steel kitchen and metal lighting systems, for example, now feature in every up-market loft catalogue. That said, it is perhaps a sign of the times that individual design classics are being substituted by far less expensive mass-produced copies from Habitat, Conran or Ikea.[2]

Each to his or her own, however. After all, the whole point about loft living is to exercise freedom of choice.

Working with light sources: a way of taking control in the loft.

Loft **dwellers**

Modes of urban living change over time and it is the architect and interior designer's task to assess new needs and adapt the human habitat accordingly. Lofts have been with us for many years and have proved capable of responding to changing **social conditions**. A recent survey in France, for example, revealed that some 55 per cent of citizens would welcome 'more modular living conditions that are adaptable to changing family circumstances, job mobility and ageing, without [this author's emphasis added] *having to move house*'.[1]
With the proliferation of new technologies, working from home is becoming increasingly common. What is more, family structures are less rigid than 50 years ago. The **flexibility** of loft living is well-suited to working from home, perhaps using a foldaway desk or a curtained-off office area. The loft's ability to metamorphose at will makes it a unique habitat able to respond promptly and effectively to new lifestyles and modern-day living in general.
Sociologist Gérard Mermet argues that 'today's consumers are more and more difficult to pin down. Traditional socio-demographic criteria such as gender,

1 - *Le Moniteur*, October 1999.

The loft provides a way of open family living. The children have their area to protect.

The parents retain their privacy behind sheer curtains.

The loft works in the same way as a house as regards responding to the demands of nature and of family life.

SIECLE

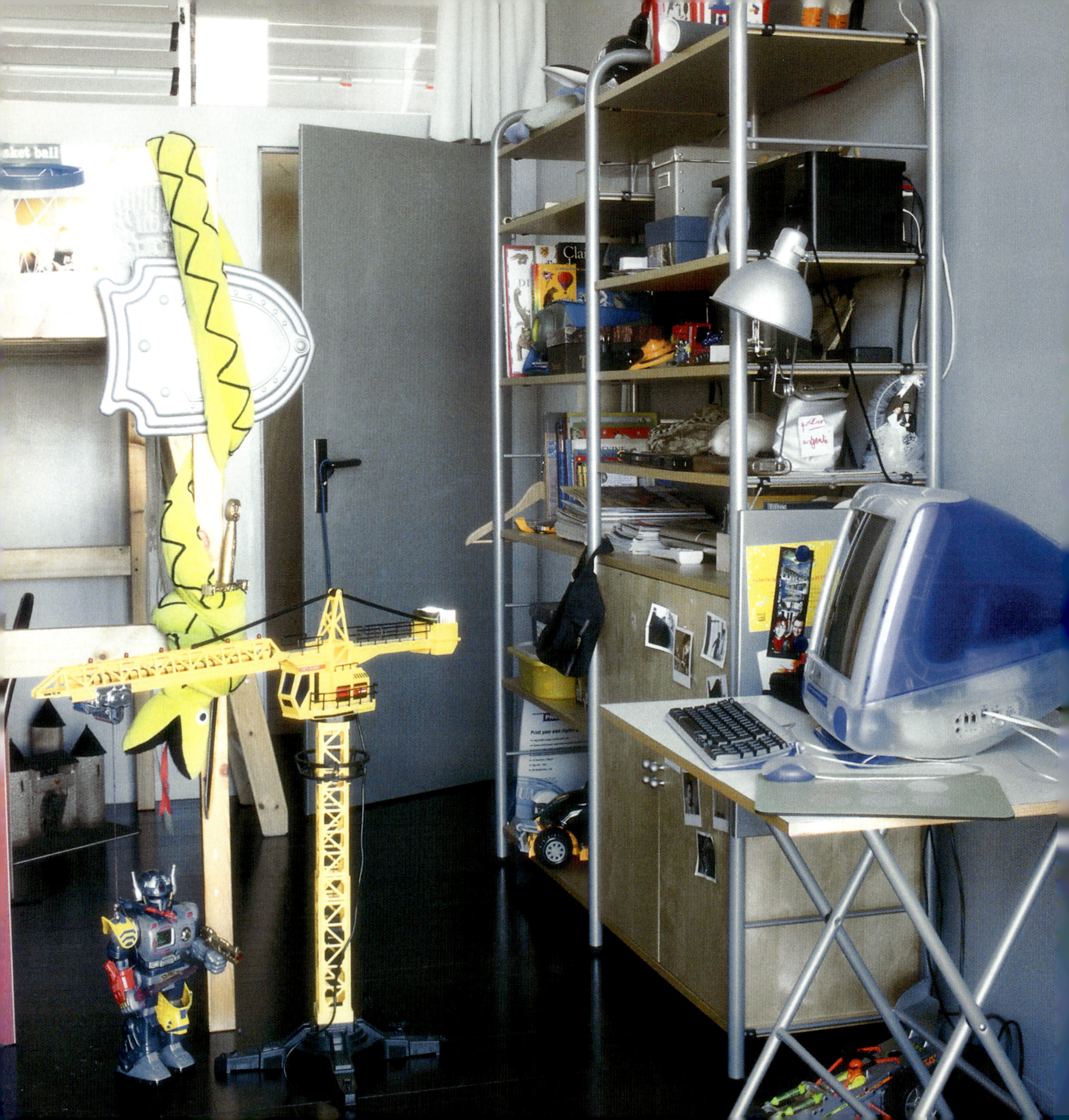

family circumstances or net monthly income are progressively less indicative of their behaviour. It follows that it is vital to start thinking of them as individuals rather than as consumers.'[1] As far as loft dwellers are concerned, Mermet's point is well taken. There is no such thing as a **stereotypical** loft dweller. Nonetheless, over the past decade, it is fair to say that lofts are typically acquired by those in the 30 to 40 age bracket who have substantial purchasing power, given that lofts are thin on the ground and, as a consequence, expensive. On the other hand, the loft pioneers who moved in 25 years ago are living proof that this type of lifestyle is not dictated by age.

On the whole, singles and couples appear to be the most adventurous when it comes to loft living. Cédric Resche of Ateliers, Lofts & Associés explains why, stating: 'A family loft has to be large and, by implication, will be more expensive. Furthermore, the loft tends to favour reception areas over sleeping quarters. Finding the right loft configuration is anything but easy.' This is not to suggest, of course, that **family life** and loft living are mutually exclusive, only that certain adjustments have to be made, possibly to create closed-off rooms for the children (reverting in the process to a more traditional style of living). Take the case of Hubert Pierre, a Paris-based painter and graphic designer, his psychiatrist wife and their two children, who says, 'We didn't know what to expect but we were worried that the noise might disturb the kids. Six years on, however, we know we made the right choice. We can live our adult life and the kids have their own intimate space'.

1 - François Bellanger: *Habitat(s): Questions et hypothèses sur l'évolution de l'habitat* ('Habitat(s): Questions and Hypotheses on the Evolution of the Human Habitat'), Éditions de l'Aube, 2000, p. 17.

Loft-buyers are changing. Couples and families want to live in lofts, as well as single people.

Other loft dwellers take the view that loft living has brought them closer together. 'We can cut ourselves off if we feel like it but, generally speaking, we can't help seeing more of each other now that we live in an open-plan area', says one. From the very beginning, lofts appealed to those in the **'creative' occupations** – artists, certainly, but also graphic designers, architects, publicists, film producers, photographers, musicians, DJs and the like. As of the 1980s, representatives of more 'traditional' professions – lawyers, bankers, brokers and others, all of them generally well-off and all of them normally associated with a more 'sedate' lifestyle – began to consider the loft living alternative. Cédric

Resche explains: 'The fact is, people who live in lofts are first and foremost people who like the good life, who like having fun. Buying a loft is often a spontaneous decision. Love at first sight – *a coup de coeur*, as we say in France'. A loft is by definition **unique**, if only to the extent that no set standards or norms apply, and the decision

to acquire one can be motivated by any number of factors: a spur-of-the-moment impulse, a genuine *coup de cœur* (as Cédric Resche describes it) or perhaps for professional reasons, or simply because a loft offers an opportunity to express oneself and one's character. For film producer and photo advertising executive Elisabeth Zacharias, it was simply 'an adventure waiting to happen'. As she explains, 'I wasn't fabulously wealthy, far from it, and I didn't have a fortune to spend. But I went for it, just the same. For me, loft living was not so much a luxury as a leap of faith, I guess'. For Zacharias, as for so many others, the loft alternative doesn't smack of elitism: it is far

rather an attitude, a lifestyle choice. In the final analysis, buying a loft comes down to an **investment in one's self** that is limited to the true believer. Axel Epifanie, who directs a centre for multimedia training, lives with his lawyer girlfriend in a former factory with very high glass ceilings. He explains why: 'We looked at all sorts of places and they were all either too stolid or too expensive, so we decided to take the plunge and invest in something that was *really* different. We took a gamble without thinking too much about it. And it paid off. We loved our loft the moment we saw it. Regrets? No, not all, although I have to admit there are one or two things – surface irritants, you might say – that we hadn't anticipated up front.'

So what are 'surface irritants' and 'one or two things we hadn't anticipated up front'? Heating problems, for example? Or acoustics? Adapting to a radical change in lifestyle, perhaps? Or simply coping with the time it takes to transform a loft, not to mention the costs involved? Ateliers, Lofts & Associés has taken stock of these and other problems, declaring, 'More and more people imagine they can get by with simply furnishing a loft, that all it takes is a little bit of tinkering here and there.' Not so. Elisabeth Zacharias recalls the hard work and stress involved: 'I was the director of operations, the site foreman as it were, and I loved every minute of it, although it was genuinely exhausting'.

Lofts are not for the faint-hearted but, for those who take on a conversion project, the rewards can be substantial. **Space** is unquestionably the prime consideration and common factor. A Parisian architect who has developed a 200 m^2 (280 yd^2) loft over two floors puts it in a nutshell: 'We were looking for a vast open space with loads of light, a space we could revamp as we saw fit. We were seduced by the loft's volume and spaciousness rather than by its residual industrial aesthetic'.

For some, the broad expanse of uncluttered space and the high ceilings have a soothing, Zen-like quality, while others simply welcome the opportunity to indulge in unusual or incongruous pursuits. New York designer Eugene Tsai gets his kicks playing basketball and Pierre Hubert and his children

Above: *Roofs often offer the possibility of creating a terrace, making the most of a view over the town.*

Left and opposite: *You can organise your way of living to match your own preferences: integrated storage to suit the minimalistic style of loft living, or having everything on show.*

enjoy indoor roller blading or the occasional game of soccer. Clearly, loft living is not simply for painters and artists: the loft can be all things to all men. It has become a symbol, a means of proclaiming one's personal identity as part of a 'switched-on' generation. By occupying a space tailored to their individual needs and preferences, loft dwellers put a personal stamp on their habitat. For Eugene Tsai, that is the crux: 'I like designing my own personal space and the loft is a virgin canvas that allows me to do precisely that'. Elisabeth Zacharias echoes this. 'My loft is "me" more than any other place I've ever lived', she says. And a Berlin stage designer living in Kreuzberg affirms that 'living in a completely open-

plan loft gives me a sense of being in control, a chance to give full expression to my individuality'.

'Personalising' is crucial, even in the case of ready-made 'turn-key' lofts that tend to appeal to well-heeled clients. In essence, a loft must seduce the prospective occupant and encourage him or her to put a personal imprint on it.

The loft's appeal is instant and intense. Cédric Resche recalls selling a loft to an American client: 'He loved it so much', says Resche, 'that he insisted on buying it all, even down to the bed linen'.

You can choose to have everything on show or hide everything away. Here, white doors hide storage solutions, the TV and even a door.

Living
the loft life

Wooden panels divide up the space without shutting off areas behind high walls.

Space, flexibility, continuity – a loft can offer all that and much more besides. But it is also a territory that is often **shared**. Strictly speaking, a loft is no longer a loft when it has been partly closed off or sub-divided. This poses a number of problems, including that of privacy and intimacy. The open-plan loft imposes its own peculiar set of rules in this respect. In essence, each occupant shares his or her space, keeping a weather eye open on the everyday needs of others.

Above: *the kitchen is no longer hidden away: it's part of the communal living area.*

Opposite: *the size of a loft space permits all kinds of fantasies: you can display a particular item you're passionate about, for instance.*

DUCATI
Desmo
Agip
DUCATI
888
MICHELIN

Psychologist and sociologist Monique Eleb sees the absence of dividing walls as a central factor influencing our perceptions of loft living. First off, she postulates **volume as a synonym of beauty** to the extent that an unbroken spatial perspective suggests a feeling of freedom. This is the loft dweller's pride and joy, the ultimate pleasure of inhabiting an endless space; a vacuum, as opposed to the sense of confinement that pervades an apartment.

Eleb also identifies a heightened self-awareness among loft dwellers. They are on an ego-trip of sorts. Spaciousness is beautiful but also prestigious. In social terms, it proclaims the loft owner to be modern in outlook, having opted for an – at times difficult but nonetheless exclusive – alternative lifestyle as featured in all the best magazines; a lifestyle that proclaims taste, refinement and 'class'. As any psychologist will readily confirm, the human habitat implies more than simply a roof over one's head: it is a mirror of one's personality (and what could be more narcissistic than loft living?).

Open-plan loft living is also a metaphor for openness of mind and spirit, a readiness to conceal nothing, to put everything on show. To a degree, it is a reprise of the Utopian communes of the 1960s and 1970s. Within the loft's four walls, it is possible to share and share alike. However: **can one genuinely share everything?** Western sensibilities are such that, for example, we do not share the intimacy that exists in Japan, where an entire family may find it quite normal to sleep together in one room. This cultural difference is one that is highly relevant to loft living. At issue are intimacy and a sense of territoriality. Everyone needs a bolt hole, a **personal space** to retreat to for a variety of reasons – to indulge one's own passions or simply to get away from the pressures of day-to-day life.

Securing a personal space in a communal setting equates first and foremost to a need to escape from judgemental and other constraints. It is a question of balancing intimacy and sporadic antipathy. In the final analysis (and despite the fact that we live in societies that are relatively free from external threat) there is a strong desire in each of us to be happy with our own company, to be alone in a protected space. Once territory has been staked out in this way, the potential for friction is correspondingly greater.

Opposite: *a bed-head also becomes a partition, hiding a cupboard or a wash-basin.*

In an open-plan space, defining one's territory may be a tenuous intellectual exercise rather than a practical process. Thus, space defined around an individual object or a particular perspective – a view, perhaps – may be sufficient to create a 'feel-good' factor. Indeed, the relative talents of architects and designers are often judged by their ability to meet the conflicting demands of security and social interaction within a common space.

It must be added that some activities are, by preference, not carried out in front of strangers. We do not always wish to be seen or observed. Where a front door opens on to an entire reception area, the whole is immediately exposed, including perhaps a disorderly kitchen space or an untidy bathroom installed at the far end. Accordingly, there is a perceived need to retain a **sense of privacy and propriety**, something not immediately achievable in the loft context. Some form of 'separation' is required, preferably without introducing fully fledged partitions that would dilute the loft's integrity.

Loft dwellers have come up with a wide range of inventive solutions in this regard. Semi-dividers, sliding doors, box constructions mounted on piles, and raised islands have been introduced to delineate zones for sleeping, sexual activities, ablutions, hobbies, professional activities and so on. These separating elements mark off individual zones of activity and create new focal points and pathways without subverting the space as a whole. The 'pathways' are, of course, virtual, created perhaps by using furniture or objects to define individual zones

Privacy can be difficult to achieve in a loft. Apart from hidden storage solutions (there's space for storage under a foldaway bed), everything is visible.

of activity, affording occupants a sense of order and a feeling of security.

As noted previously, the re-converted loft is and always has been a place in which to live and work. Premises once given over to manual labour now host new production and design industries. The advent of information technology and the exponential growth in telecommunications have resulted in work no longer being restricted to one physical space. The loft has emerged as the ideal **spacious and cost-effective inner-city** site for start-up enterprises, where architects, designers, musicians and others can set up a practice, build a sound studio, install an office or provide meeting facilities.

Managing living and working space can still be problematic, however. Defining and delineating space is achieved in many instances by the simple expedient of using a curtained-off area or even a piece of office furniture to define a working or living zone, but the bottom line is that living and working areas will inevitably impinge one on the other to some degree. **Fusion** (or 'confusion', perhaps) will occur. Interior designer Felicity Bell, who has transformed her loft space to create a meeting room and an office for her assistant, points out: 'Our work is such an integral part of our life that complete separation of the two is a sheer impossibility'.[1] Painter Pierre Hubert meanwhile has opted for a screen that he uses both to hang his canvases and, on the reverse, as a storage element. He is quick to concede that his private life can be disruptive in terms of his work, saying: 'There is often a risk of one interfering with the other and causing a distraction'.

That may be so, but the great majority of loft dwellers insist that the absence of dividers is conducive to that

all-important sense of **freedom**. 'The openness is liberating', says Elisabeth Zacharias, adding that it is also 'more efficient'. An architect couple in New York have elected to locate their office in the totally open-plan centre of their loft. 'That way, we can swap ideas with each other as and whenever we like, from the bathroom or the kitchen or wherever', they say.

The media may often elect to portray loft living as superficial and snobbish, but the simple fact is that the loft is, first and foremost, a place where people can create and communicate.

1 - Marcus Field, Mark Irving: *Lofts*, Seuil, 1999.

A terrace provides extra space as an extension to the loft.

Material considerations

The construction materials that define twentieth-century living have precious little in common with the components celebrated by the Arts and Crafts movement at the latter end of the nineteenth century. Although very varied, the former are, generally speaking, industry-based, whereas the latter were drawn predominantly from nature. Even so, the two are united by a common bond, namely a concern for 'honest beauty'.

The emergence of reinforced concrete, stee glass, rubber and so on has yielded new arch tectural forms. At the same time, synthetics suc as plastic and its derivatives (polypropylen PVC, polycarbonates, etc.) have made hug inroads into everyday domestic life. Over tim industrially developed products such as thes have become accepted as materials in the sens that the distinction between the artificial and th natural, the industrial and the domestic, has bee progressively eroded.

Wood

Wood is widely available, versatile and easily worked. As such, it is the construction material *par excellence*. Today, the term 'wood' is applied to a broad spectrum of manufactured products, including hardboard, chipboard, laminates and MDF in all their variants – as panels, floorboards, planks, beams and so on.

It is estimated that there are some 40,000 species of wood and that we currently use a third of those from one of two broad groups: the resinous group (including pine, spruce, fir and sequoia) or the broad-leaf group (mahogany, birch, beech, oak, maple). The former group is cheap but soft, and requires

treatment to prevent rotting, whereas the latter is usually known as hard wood and comes in a wide choice of colours and textures. Wood is readily recycled and the worn and patinated appearance of certain types of old wood is very much in demand. This includes old wooden strip flooring, beams and roofing timbers, all of which are given a second lease on life in the loft context (without, let it be said, any need for refurbishing).

Wood can be used in an infinite number of ways. The common use is for flooring, but other standard applications are for work surfaces, wall cladding, shelving and, of course, furniture (including, now, Japanese-style bathrooms). Not least, wood can be treated and finished in a variety of ways, including waxing and French polishing or with the application of oils, paints, varnishes, lacquers and veneers.

HOLZER

Stone

Stone is another essential and highly versatile construction material. Marble, granite, slate and sandstone can be hewn and fashioned into blocks, worktops, staircases, wash basins and the like and can also serve as a decorative alternative to wall coverings. Stone comes in soft and hard variants, both dry and porous. It is heavy and, as a result, requires underpinning by stout beams to accommodate its weight. When used as a floor covering,

it amplifies sound. A large variety of finishes can be used (polished, sanded down, granulated, reconstituted, etc.), depending on whether the final result is meant to be modern or rustic. Certain types of stone (notably slate and sandstone), are resilient and wear particularly well, whereas others gradually discolour or take on a patina over time. Another salient feature of stone is price: it rarely comes cheap.

Concrete

Le Corbusier and others must take credit fc introducing concrete as one of the essenti building blocks of twentieth-century archite ture. Today, concrete tends to be regarde as a second-rate material, although its simp untreated surface appearance is still assoc ated with certain avant-garde interiors. Whe used for floors and walls, concrete imparts distinctly industrial look to any building.

Concrete is obtained from a mixture varying proportions of cement, sand ar water which, depending on the respectiv quantities used, determines the quality the surface finish and its propensity to crac or degrade. Concrete is porous and col it amplifies sound, discolours readily ar requires waterproofing if it is to last. On th other hand, its habitually grey colour ca be alleviated by the addition of pigments. polished, however, concrete loses its typical rough and minimalist look.

Metal

ı the early days, cast iron and steel were sed almost exclusively for bearing elements in ıdustrial buildings, notably for support beams nd decorative girders. Today, however, metls exhibit a flexibility and a multiplicity of use ıat lend themselves to a wide number of rchitectural features. Steel substrate can be eated in various ways – polished, brushed, rooved, patterned, coated or otherwise surce-finished – to accommodate an almost infite range of professional design applications.

Aluminium is a metal that is finding increasing favour for use in stairways, mezzanines and other platforms. It has certain drawbacks, however, notably its poor acoustics and the fact that it is an aesthetically 'cold' medium.

Zinc, once considered mainly as a top protective layer for iron and steel, has acquired a new image, not least among loft dwellers who are drawn increasingly to its natural patina and who currently use it for wall coverings, worktops and bathroom fittings.

Glass

Glass admits light and, therefore plays a significant role in contemporary interior design. Transparency imparts a new dynamic to spatial volumes, enabling zones of activity to be discreetly highlighted. Moreover, glass surfaces reinforce the overall impression of openness towards the outside. Dividers,

floors, walkways, built-in sliding doors, these are only some of the many uses to which this versatile material can be put.

Glass can be used in its standard form or can be 'frosted' to admit light while imparting a sense of privacy. Reinforced glass, which is to say glass that contains a delicate network

of metal threads, is employed where security is paramount.

The use of glass over large surface areas can cause major temperature fluctuations in a room. Glass bricks have positive sound and heat insulation characteristics. Used as an interior design element, glass lends itself to a wide range of applications. Of late, it has been used with increasing frequency in bathrooms, where it is moulded to produce elegant sinks and wash basins.

Plastics

It is safe to say that no single material has ever invaded our daily lives so swiftly and to such a degree as plastic, a modern material that hovers somewhere between Pop Art and Kitsch. Nevertheless, whether opaque, translucent, coloured, rigid or supple, plastics are nothing if not versatile. They appear capable of responding to the widest possible spectrum of design applications.

Plastic materials such as Altuglass, Dacryl, polyethylene, polyvinyl chloride, polypropylene, melamine and polycarbonates are manufactured using the polymerisation process and have emerged in many instances as useful substitutes for other materials such as glass and wood. Plastics are used for anything and everything, it seems – from floor coverings to domestic utensils.

An innovation in the loft: a water feature creates a comforting and living dimension in a space that can sometimes be rather cold.

Walda Pairon

Acknowledgements

The authors' grateful thanks go to Monique Eleb, psychologist, sociologist, lecturer on architecture at the College of Paris-Malaquais and author of several studies on the evolution of the human habitat and lifestyles in France; to psychologist and author François Vigouroux; and to Colette, Anne, Francis, Eugène, Denis, Mathieu and the staff at Ateliers, Lofts & Associés [www.ateliers-lofts.com].

The editor's grateful thanks go to the following for their participation:

Monsieur Alary / Architect Daniel Villotte
Monsieur Marc Corbiau / Owner and architect
Monsieur Axel Epifanie
Monsieur and Madame Godivier / Owner and architect
Madame Rose Holzer / Owner and architect
Monsieur Jean-Cédric Jacmart / Architect Atelier 20
Monsieur Thierry Lamoine
Monsieur Luc Pérénom and Madame Véronique Decruck
Monsieur and Madame Hubert Pierre / Architect Monsieur Eric Parisis
Madame Andrée Putman / Owner and architect
Monsieur Jean-Marc Vynckier / Owner and architect
Madame Elisabeth Zacharias / Architect Monsieur François Muracciole

And architects:

Claude Morphée: pp. 40, 41, 42-43.
Pierre Roch: pp. 20, 80, 81 t. and b., 86-87, 89, 100 b., 110 mr., 112.

And many thanks to Bruno Degoul, editorial assistant.

Photographic credits

Corbis
The Brett Weston Archive 8-9 – *Angelo Hornak* 12-13 – *G.E. Kidder Smith* 11.

Marc Domage
24-25, 26-27, 28-29, 36, 38, 44, 45, 50-51, 71, 72, 73, 107.

Frédéric Ducout
35 r., 47, 56, 57, 58, 90 t. and b., 91 t., 94, 95 t. and b., 100 t., 101 b., 103, 104, 105 t. and b., 109 b., 111 m., 113 b.

Inside
14-15, 18-19, 21, 96-97, 98-99.

Laurent Teisseire
cover., 4, 6-7, 10, 16-17, 20, 22, 23 t. and b., 30, 31, 32, 33, 34, 35 l., 37, 39 t., 39 b., 40, 41, 42-43, 46, 48, 49, 52, 53 t. and b., 54, 55, 58, 59, 60-61, 62, 63, 64, 65, 66, 67, 68 t. and b., 69, 70, 76 t. and b., 77, 78, 79, 80, 81 t. and b., 82, 83, 84, 85, 86, 87, 88, 89, 91 b., 92, 93, 100 b., 101 t. and m., 102, 106 t. and b., 108, 109 tl. and r., 110, 111 t. and b., 112, 113 ml. and mr.

Every effort has been made to obtain the necessary rights and permissions. The publisher should be notified of any errors or omissions and these will be corrected in subsequent editions.